This is me!

I Wrote This Book about You!

Created By:

Year: ----------

The Life Graduate Publishing Group

We love to receive reviews from our customers. If you had the opportunity to provide a review we would greatly appreciate it. Thank you!

Copyright 2020 - The Life Graduate Publishing Group

No part of this book may be scanned, reproduced or distributed in any printed or electronic form without the prior permission of the author or publisher.

ABOUT THE AUTHOR

My Name :

My Age :

I wrote this book about you because :

I LOVE YOU BECAUSE....

THIS IS A TRACE OF MY HAND

Place your hand here and trace around it with a pencil

MY FAVORITE PLACE TO VISIT WITH YOU IS.....

_____

_____

_____

_____

_____

_____

You like to relax by doing this.. *RELAX*

_____

_____

_____

_____

_____

_____

THIS IS MY FAVORITE PHOTO OF US

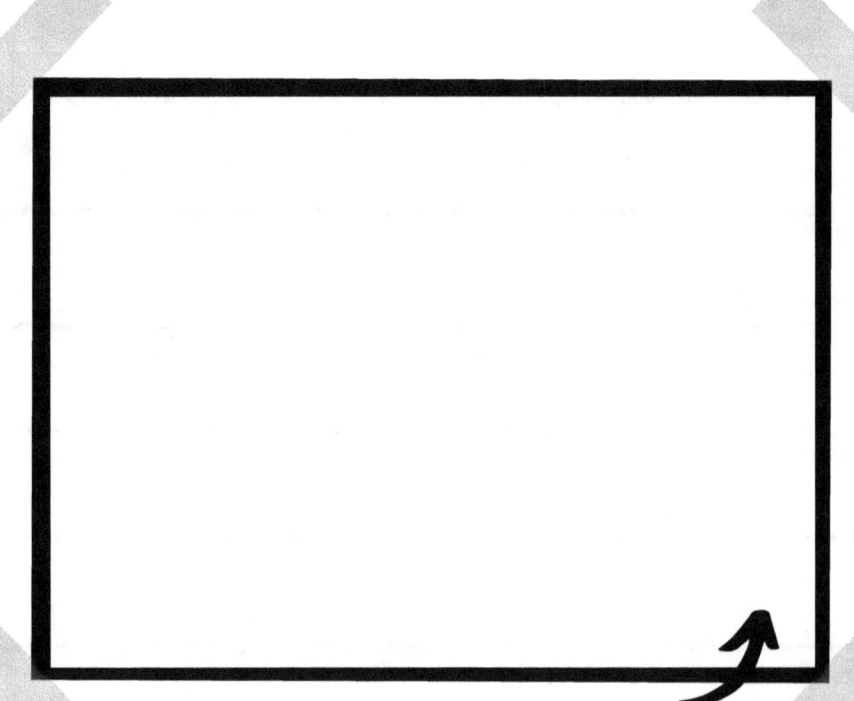

Stick your favorite photo here!

THIS IS A DRAWING OF US TOGETHER

These are 3 things you do that are kind.

1. _____

2. _____

3. _____

We celebrate your birthday on..

MONTH _____

DAY _____

I love birthday cake!!

You cook the best......

My favorite story you have told me was...

I love Stories!!

I'm very brave but... I still get a little scared when...

I would like you to show me how to...

Your favorite time of the year is...

because....

This is a drawing of us together at..

I think you are the best at....

Your favorite food is.....

If I could get you anything in the whole wide world it would be...

I hope that one day we can......

I think you look like

from the T.V !

If I designed a T-Shirt for you, it would say this...

My Special Design!

You taught me how to.....

You can do this better than anyone else!

SPECIAL MOMENTS

Add other special photo's or drawings here

SPECIAL MOMENTS

Add other special photo's or drawings here

THIS HAS BEEN MY SPECIAL GIFT THAT I HAVE CREATED FROM ME TO YOU. I HOPE YOU LIKE IT!

My autograph

A Selection Of Other Books In The Series

www.thelifegraduate.com